Decoding SEO the Easy Way:

How to Become an Expert in SEO No Time

By Michelle Blake

Published by WE CANT BE BEAT LLC

Krob817@yahoo.com

Table of Contents

Introduction to SEO

SEO is probably the most used acronym in this modern era. All of us know that SEO means Search Engine Optimization. Why is SEO important? It's important because individuals, businesses, and big industries survive and thrive on SEO. You either use SEO to your advantage or die.

Everyone has a website. Some websites draw eyeballs while some simply languish in the background. Some people believe that you can simply design a fabulous website and you are done – people will visit your site, buy the stuff out there and you will become a millionaire. The truth is that you have to market your website first. How do you market a website? How do you create visibility? How many ways are there to make your website presence felt? There is only one – SEO.

Your goal, aim and sole purpose should be to get your website figure on the first page of search results. If you estimate the number of search results in the vicinity of millions, you can guess the probability of your website appearing on the first page. Almost nil. However there are websites which find themselves on the first page by beating all odds. How do they achieve this miracle? Of course it seems like a miracle.

From shoes to submarines, everything can be sold on the internet provided you know the secret of selling online. SEO or Search Engine Optimization is a huge part of this secret. Understanding SEO is therefore critical to your online success.

Google is the biggest, largest and fattest search engine – whether you like it or not. Bing and Yahoo are   competitors who really don't matter much. Your focus therefore must be on Google search engine. You may like to know that Bing and Yahoo follow a search algorithm similar to Google. What is a search algorithm? You will learn more about it later in this book. First let's look at an example.

John had inherited a shoe shop. The shop was strategically located and experienced thousands of footfalls during the day. For every hundred visitors, two to three converted into sales – a good percentage when compared to other traditional footwear outlets. John however was more ambitious. He wanted to increase sales dramatically. He was told that a website would bring customers from across the world. John wondered how a website could change fortunes so dramatically. He calculated that a website would cost him no more than a few hundred dollars, including cost of design, development and maintenance. He took the risk and gave a green signal to the project. The shoe website was launched within two months. The site was attractive and better than the competitors. John waited excitedly for a surge in traffic to his website which unfortunately never happened. It was natural for John to blame the website designer. He thought that some critical feature must be missing which stopped people from visiting his website. The website designer threw up his hands claiming that the website did everything which it was required to do. Getting traffic was not part of his job. John wondered aloud as to whose job it was to attract traffic?

John is not an isolated case of misplaced confidence. People simply assume that launching a website is sufficient to attract eyeballs. The truth is that you have to sell your website like you sell everything else. How do you sell a website? You optimize your website and make it available to others for viewing. This can only be achieved if your website appears in search results or more specifically on the first page of search results. This book will teach you the secret of SEO.

Let's look at SEO from a different perspective. Imagine that you were hunting for a bargain online. You are specifically interested in buying shoes. What do you do? You search for 'shoes' on Google. Within seconds you are confronted by a million sites selling shoes. Do you go to the second page of search results? You probably don't. Most people restrict themselves to the results on the first page. Now pay attention to the websites which have shown up. What if the results have nothing to do with shoes? What if the results were leading you to porn sites instead? Maybe you won't mind but usually people will get frustrated and avoid using Google search in future. This is the reason why Google makes sure that you get relevant search results. By relevance we mean finding sites on 'shoes' when you search for shoes. How does Google ensure that you find relevant results? Google has spent millions of dollars finding the right algorithm or mathematical formula which discovers and connects your search word with websites. This is obviously keyword search.

Now put yourself in the shoes of the person searching for 'Shoes'. What should you do to get Google search to show you in search results? It's simple – you have to create relevance. Google does not reveal its search algorithm. It's a secret which no one is aware of, otherwise people will try and game the system. However, Google does leak some important aspects of its search engine to the public. From these small drips and dribbles, SEO experts have found a way to create relevance. This book is written specifically to reveal these secrets.

Google algorithm is not a static formula. It is evolving and changing continuously. You must understand that people use 'black hat' techniques to game the search system. For example, back links were once considered to be an important part of SEO. Slowly people started creating backlinks from meaningless sites. Thousands of Link farms sprung up all over the internet. You could buy backlinks by the dozen and get your website to rank high in search results. Obviously Google refused to accept this situation – their reputation was at stake. As a result, google tweaked its search engine to identify link farms. These links were ignored when ranking websites. Link farms disappeared overnight after Google introduced the changes.

You will learn about various SEO white hat or ethical techniques in this book. You will be able to dominate search results by using the secret sauce which you learn to mix into your website. Here it is on how to decode SEO the right way to become an expert in no time.

Chapter 1 - On page and off page SEO

SEO means optimizing your site for search engines. When you hit the search button after entering a word or phrase as a query, the search engine goes into overdrive. You can't hear it whirring because everything happens in the background. This whirring is cause by the search algorithm which dives into a list of websites which are likely to provide the right content with respect to your search keyword. This algorithm is based on two main factors – relevancy and authority. What does this mean?

You might have noticed that most of the times, whenever you use a search engine, the Wikipedia page always crops up. Why does this happen? Does Google have some understanding with the website owner? Some underhand ploy? You will agree that you will always find the right information on Wikipedia, whatever may be your search word or keyword. Can we say that Wikipedia site is relevant? Yes. What about other relevant sites? Your won site may be equally relevant but unfortunately Google does not agree with your opinion. The most important factor which Wikipedia has is authority. In essence Wikipedia has both relevancy and authority. How do you position your website to be both relevant and authoritative?

Relevancy and Onsite SEO

Onsite means whatever is happening within your website. You must provide sufficient reason for Google to consider you as a relevant website. The first step in this direction would be to make your content relevant. Google, for that matter any search engine, is not human. It's an algorithm which tries to mimic human intelligence. It cannot differentiate between a scientific paper and a homemade recipe. But it has a great memory. It finds the keywords associated with your web page and stores this information including the number of times it appears on the web page in its memory. There was a time when SEO experts simply loaded a web page with keywords. For example, the keyword 'shoe' would be repeated a hundred times on a web page making it most relevant. Google saw through the sham and introduced something called keyword density. If a keyword exceeded a certain number the web page would be red flagged by the Google search engine.

Keyword density became an important part of onsite SEO. By the latest count 2 to 3% keyword density seems to be acceptable to Google. Onsite SEO also takes into consideration how the content is structured. The page title and other factors (which we will discuss later) are factored into the Google algorithm to decide relevancy of your web page.

Now, there may be hundreds of web pages which may be equally relevant. Keyword density alone cannot be the sole criteria to judge which pages should appear in SERPs (Search Engine Results Page).

Note: Why is Google picky about the whole process? Why not dump search results into the

SERP? This is a good question which bothers many people, especially those who are new to SEO. The answer is really very simple. Imagine that you search for ' Shoes' and you get results which have a vague connection with 'Shoes'. If this happens continuously, you will stop using Google search. What's the point you will ask. Google will no longer be a popular search engine. Within a year, Google will end up broke and may have to shut its operations. Now you know why Google tries its hardest to show the most relevant results – their life depends on it. When it's a question of life and death, you better be careful. Google has therefore found other ways to identify the best websites which are relevant to search keywords.

Off page SEO

You must have heard of 'Link building'? A major part of SEO consists of 'Link building'. By creating links to your website you are signaling the Google search algorithm that your site is important – other websites want to be associated with you. As a result you become an authority. Therefore you must have inbound links to satisfy Google search algorithm that you deserve or merit a mention on the first page of SERPs. It's easy to imagine that SEO guys found a way to shortcut the link philosophy. Thousands of link farms sprouted up on the internet promising instant link nirvana. You simply had to pay a few bucks and the smart guys would provide a hundred backlinks in no time. There are hundreds of guys out there trying to game the system. Big websites pay millions to SEO professionals just to enter the legion of first page SERPs. There is always the danger of getting blacklisted by Google for trying to game their algorithm. This can also happen to you and getting out of the blacklist can be tough. So, don't try to game the system. Here you will learn legitimate ways to master SEO.

As you can very well guess, Google put an end to the link farm fiasco. They modified their algorithm to only include links which came from legit sites. All the link farms disappeared overnight. Google can be ruthless sometimes.

Link building is an important part of offline SEO. Can you get a link from Wikipedia? Your website will jump the queue and land on the first page of SERPs if you can manage a link here. It's clear that you have to link to sites which have authority. There are many ay to do this besides Wikipedia.

Link building is a tedious process. Every link matters and you must be careful who you choose to link with. Some SEO experts will suggest that you get reciprocal links from authoritative sites. Google has factored this into their algorithm and the new is that you will get not more than a drop of link juice from this arrangement. You will learn more about link juice later in this book.

Why not get links from other blogs? You can launch a hundred one page blogs and put a link in each one of them. The problem with this approach is that blogs are not considered as authority sites (except a few popular blogs). You will be wasting your time and effort if you try to fool Google.

The conclusion which you reach is that SEO is pretty simple process but there are no shortcuts. If you try and game the process, Google may penalize you, which would be worse than not getting into the first page of SERPs.

Chapter 2- On page SEO secrets

Choosing and using the right keywords, page optimization using tags etc.

How Does a Website Work?

To understand SEO you must know a little about website design. As an SEO expert you must know websites like a doctor knows the human body.

To many of us a website belongs to a magical world. You can visit a site and get information, buy products and services, play games and do a lot more. How does a website work? Essentially there are two distinct parts of a website – frontend and backend.

The frontend is what you see. The web page appearing on your screen is part of the frontend with text, images and navigation buttons. The frontend is developed or designed using HTML (Hyper Text Markup language) and CSS (Cascading style sheet). Modern websites use JavaScript as well for frontend development. You need a web designer to create your web pages. The web designer uses elements like text, images and sometimes audio to put together a web page. The images are created using popular image editing software like Photoshop. The web designer may also test the site for effective user interface and ease of use.

The backend of a website is the part which is invisible to you. This part enables communication between the website and the user.

Website consists of web pages like home, about and contact us. You have to upload these web pages to a web server. You will have to hire a web server to store the web pages. This is called web hosting. You will learn about web hosting in detail later. You can design or create the web pages yourself or get a web designer to develop the web pages for you.

The web server will store your web site in memory and send to a user when they ask for it. The user is called a client and he initiates or asks for a web page using Hypertext Transfer Protocol (HTTP). The server sends HTML pages (which are a part of your website) to the client. This is the most basic model of how a website works.

How does a server identify your website? You know that websites have names like youknow.com. This name is associated with an IP address or Internet protocol address. All the devices on the internet identify each other by numbers like 124.22.23.01. The actual web address or name must therefore be converted into numbers or IP address. This is done by DNS or Domain Name System. DNS converts a domain name into IP address. Why do you need such a complicated system? Why not use IP addresses directly. Well, you could have done this except that remembering IP addresses would have been a huge task. You are more likely to remember friendly names than numbers. A DNS server converts a domain name into an IP address and sends the user to the server in which your website is hosted.

Coming back to the subject of backend, it is not enough to simply upload your files to the server. You need a process to store and retrieve information. You can use a CMS or Content Management System to manage your website which is hosted on a server.

Getting the Right Domain Name

1.   The first requirement is to choose a simple name. Sometimes you may get carried away by fancy names which seem trendy and fashionable. These oh-so-smart domain names are to be avoided at any cost.

2.   The website name or URL (Uniform Resource Locator) must be short. Long website addresses difficult and tedious to type. Users don't like to type long domain names. Moreover they can easily make a typographical error. Avoid all these issues by choosing a short name.

3.   You must know that Google loves domain names and uses it as a keyword in their search

algorithm. If you are into the shoe business, you can select a name like shoes.com. Unfortunately you will find that the name is already taken – so are shoes.org and shoes.net and shoes.info. The reason is obvious. The next best choice would be americanshoes.com which you will find to your frustration is also gone. Now you know why it's difficult to choose a simple name – they are already taken. Still you can find a name which is linked to your business. Your domain name is your business card. It tells a story. It reflects your personality. You should not be casual when choosing a domain name. Be serious. Be correct.

4.   Maybe you belong to Texas and maximum number of customers is from this area. Why not use Texas in your domain name?

5.   Do not get into the number game. For example, avoid get2publish when you can use getpublished as a domain name. Figuring out numbers in a domain name can be tiresome.

6.   Can you combine a realistic domain name which spells out your business but is yet easy to remember? This is a winning combination.

7.   Domain name extensions are as important as the domain name itself. Users directly type .com as extension without thinking. If your domain does not appear in the browser window, users will abandon search rather than look for another extension, unless they are desperate. Try and get a .com extension. It will be ideal if you can buy other alternative extensions which point to the same website.

8.   Try and think long term. Your domain name can become your trademark in future. Your company may be remembered by your domain name. You should not underestimate the power of a domain name.

9.   Avoid using registered trademarks in your domain name to avoid legal issues. Don't use popular trade names for this reason. Of course people do this intentionally to later sell their domain name for a hefty profit. This is called

domain squatting. Lately there have been many litigations over domain squatting and the courts have ruled in favor of legitimate owners. Therefore you should avoid known and popular trade names in your domain name.

10.   Avoid long domain names. Long names are difficult to remember and typical users can't remember long names. Long names are also difficult to parse by search engines.

The big picture

Optimization must be approached from the top first. The overall objective of the website has to be kept in mind before going down to details. There are many elements which must consider before implementing the nuts and bolts of SEO.

First impression is sometimes the last impression

Do you know that your website visitors leave after looking at your home page? This is called bounce rate. Your home page is the only opportunity for you to make a good impression. However, most of us tend to focus on a particular aspect of SEO and miss the obvious. Remember that you will monetize your website only if the visitors end up buying your product. Attracting visitors is important but making them stay is equally vital.

Follow the leader

It's quite easy to understand the reasons why a website works. You have to simply observe your favorite website and you will get all the answers. The first characteristic of a good website is the look which must be clean. Cluttered look is a great way to turn away visitors. You must use legible, readable fonts and paragraphs which are spaced suitably. Websites suffer from user apathy because of these reasons:

1.   Meandering and clueless navigation which leave a visitor confused about the purpose

of the website. You should not expect your website to perform several tasks at one time. Be clear about the purpose and let the visitor know what to expect.

2.   Have you noticed that some websites take ages and ages to load? What do you do when this happens? You abandon the site and start looking at other alternatives. Don't let this fate fall on your website. Make sure that the web pages of your website load quickly. Page load time is a criterion in SEO.

3.   Avoid auto-play music because this detracts from the original purpose and also causes inordinate load times.

4.   Too many redirects can spoil user experience. Avoid redirects as much as possible.

5.   Canonicalization errors can be easily excluded if you are careful.

6.   Make sure that robots.txt is present if you are looking at a website with SEO perspective. This small text file tells search engine robot

everything about a website in a nutshell. Check for the file sitemap.xml. This xml file tells search engine robot about the site hierarchy.

Keyword research

There are keywords and keywords – which of them are for you? This is a tough question to answer, till you look around. Even before you begin writing the first word of content, you must know your keywords. One the best keyword analysis tool is provided by Google .It's called "Google keyword tool". By the way, Google likes to keep things simple. If you want to get into their head, you must start thinking like them. There are other keyword research tools, both paid and free, but none come anywhere near Google keyword tool. Another assumption, which is reasonable, is that a tool made by Google must in some way tie-in with their search algorithm.

To access this tool go to http://www.googlekeywordtool.com/ and then select Google Keyword tool. This site has a number of other very important tools which you can use. By the way, this tool is provided by Google for their AdWords users but all of us can use it. You can join Google AdWords program, which is also free and access some additional information.

You would notice that there are a whole lot of things you can do with this tool. Begin with filling the keyword phrase of your interest – "making money from Home". Using a long tailed keyword or phrase is recommended because you are unlikely to run into established websites. For example, if you used only money as your keyword, you will be competing with CNN and Wikipedia which means your website will never appear on the first page of Google results. You will increase your chances of getting into the first page, if you use "making money from Home".

Notice what happens if you key-in the phrase "making money from Home". The keyword tool throws out 100 related keywords with information on competition, global monthly searches and local monthly searches. By default, the local monthly search is set to United States which can be changed by using advanced options & Filters.

For "Making money at home", you get only 165000 hits but had you used "Make money at home", you would had 246,000 hits. Now that's what Google search is all about. Using this tool you would be able to find the right keywords or phrase which you would be using on your website.

Google insights

You must use Google insights to drill further into your keywords. Now that you have the right keyword/s or phrase/s, you can move to the next stage. What is your competitor doing?

Analysis of competition

Smart businesses want to know what their competitors are doing. In management jargon it is known as assessing their strength and weaknesses. In SEO, understanding competitor's strategy is extremely helpful.

There are good competitors and bad competitors. You must compete only with the good and successful websites. In SEO this means websites which rank high in Google search results. How do you assess performance of competitors? How do you understand their keyword strategy? How do you know about their web traffic? These inputs can hasten your progress towards website optimization. Let's face it. You don't have to reinvent the wheel. If someone has done it successfully, you must not hesitate to follow in their footsteps. Here are a couple of ways by which you can gather intelligence.

1.   Look into their HTML code

This is perhaps the easiest way to analyze your competitor's website. You don't have to know any coding or be a software engineer. This is how you do it. From the toolbar in Internet Explorer, click on view and then on source.

This provides you with some interesting observations. Notice that the Title tag is the same as the article heading and the description has the first line of the article. This means that your Title tag and description should also follow the same format. You can get more information reading the site by analyzing the source of a web page.

2.   **Look at Alexa Ranking**

Alexa is a great source of information on competitor's traffic. But more importantly, you can get complete information on their inbound links.

The traffic rank and number of links are available. Similar data can be obtained with regard to your competitors.

Keyword optimization of content

Now that you have the keyword/s or phrase/s, you have to now look at your content. By content we mean articles, web page content and any other written material. One of the things you must be careful about is to develop or write content only after selecting the right keywords after research. Often, website owners first get their website up and running and then think about optimization. This temptation must be avoided. Remember that your keyword is now "Make money at home", which had the highest hits - 246,000.

Where to insert keywords?

Most of us assume that placing keywords anywhere within the content is fine. This is another fallacy. Research has shown that keyword placement has a critical role to play in search engine optimization. The rules are as follows-

Use H1 and H2 tags

What are H1 and H2 tags? These are the headings you use inside your content. In a way it is natural to use headings to convey what to expect in the coming paragraph. Speed readers scan the heading and move on without reading subsequent text. Google developers lean heavily on human psychology. Their crawler or Bot is likely to follow the same pattern or logic as a speed reader would. This makes Headers extremely important. We will be discussing Title tag later on, but enough to say that the Header must be the same as your title, with the keywords. Google SEO experts swear by this formula and therefore highly recommended.

Where to place keywords inside the content?

Keywords must be placed in the first as well as last 50 words of content. The last 50 words would generally be a conclusion and therefore merits keyword placement. More keywords can be sprinkled within the content.

Use of more than one keyword in a web page

The temptation is obvious. We would like to stuff our content with as many keywords as possible. The problem with this approach is that the content invariably looks stilted and reads badly.

For example, if we use "Make money at home' as well as "Making money from home", the content will contain nothing but these two phrases. The likelihood of Google crawler getting thoroughly confused is high. This may damage your chances of ranking high on search results. The best way to negotiate such a situation is to optimize two web pages, one each for one keyword. By doing this you would be able to optimize your pages for both the keywords without attracting penalty.

Keyword density

What is the ideal percentage of keywords? This question needs to be looked at from human angle. In any normal text, how many times would you encounter the same words? Google has concluded that 2-3% is normal. You don't need extensive research to come to this conclusion. More than 3-4% would be termed as keyword stuffing. This was a common feature before Google became the foremost search engine.

How much of content is enough?

Google wants to see websites filled with content. There are reports that websites having fewer than 100 pages is considered skeletal by Google. But most of the websites don't really need 100 pages. Does it mean that they won't rank well on search results? This seems to be the case. What can you do to increase pages? One of the ways is to provide articles, technical reports and such documents as web content. If you have hundred such documents, your website would look decent in the eyes of Google Bot. Make sure that you keep within keyword density guidelines for each page. One advantage of having hundred pages is that you can target four or five keywords – one keyword for every 20 pages.

Web page design, site navigation and HTML tags

You have researched and chosen the keywords, looked at competitors and created suitable content with these keywords. Now you can design your website. Design doesn't mean the look and feel but from SEO standpoint.

First, we will create suitable HTML tags for all the web pages. There is no need to get worried at this stage. You don't have to be a software expert to do this.

Every web page is essentially an HTML page. It has a certain layout and format – just like a "Microsoft Word" page.

From SEO standpoint there are three tags which you need to know. These are Title, Description and Keyword tags. Out of these the keyword tag has now become redundant. Google no longer uses Keyword tag and therefore it's of no use to us.

The Title tag informs users about the web page. It actually appears at the top of any web page. This Title tag must have your keywords .As discussed earlier it is desirable to have the Title same as the web page heading. This gives a positive signal to Google crawler. The Title tag must be less than 60 characters and more than 50. Title tag is a part of HTML and must be provided to the website designer to be inserted by them.

The Description tag is the next important element of a web page. This describes what the web page is likely to contain. Once again there must be coherence between Title tag, Description tag, Web page heading and the content. This gives a strong signal to Google Bot which indexes the page. Description should not exceed 160 characters and must be above 150 characters. No one is going to penalize you if you exceed or fall short but Google does keep track of such stuff and will inform you about the size. We will discuss later how Google reports such events.

Links within the website or internal link must also contain the keywords which are relevant to web pages to which they link. You must ensure that you use text links as opposed to images, since Google Bot cannot recognize images. In some cases you may want to use images. In that case you must also provide text links additionally. These links would be for consumption of Google Bot. This would form a part of site navigation.

You may provide this material to the web designer who would use your guidelines. There is no need for additional information since you have specified all aspects of SEO.

Putting it together – webmaster tools

What have you done till now?

1. Keyword research to discover the right keywords

2. Competitor analysis to refine keyword strategy

3. Created content with 2-3% keyword density

4. Created Meta tags for Title, Description

5. Using the above information you have hosted your website.

There is one more step which is required to enable Google crawler to visit your site. Some people assume that Google would on its own visit your site and index it. This is however not the case. You have to submit your site to Google. Google recommends that you provide your website information in xml format. This is called sitemap. Once you have created a sitemap you are ready to submit your website to Google.

You must now submit your site through Google Webmaster tools. You need a gmail account to do this. Create a free gmail account and go to http://www.google.com/webmasters/. This is the most important part of the entire exercise. Here Google will tell you all you want to know about your site. It is probably the most useful and critical tool for website analysis.

You can submit your website here. It takes a couple of days for the Google crawler to visit your site. Once your site is indexed, the webmaster tool will tell you everything about your site. Broken links, size of Title and Description tags, external link issues are more common and need to be corrected. You can resubmit your site after correcting the problems.

Summing up

There is one thing which you must have noticed. Your SEO strategy is now top down and there is coherence throughout your site. When the Google crawler looks at your site, it finds a uniform keyword policy. There is continuity in your title, description, heading along with content and internal link text. The Google Bot will be able to analyze and suitably index your site for specific keywords.

By following the above strategy, you would be sending a strong signal to Google – that your website is worth a first page ranking.

Chapter 3 - Off page SEO secrets

On page SEO means keyword optimization in a nutshell. You want to tell the search engine that your site offers content for so-and-so keyword. Imagine that you have done this successfully. You have managed to get the attention of Google. That by itself is a huge step. But wait a minute. How does Google know that your website is dependable? How does it know that your source of information is reliable? How do you prove to Google that you deserve a mention on the first page of search results or SERP's?

The three most important factors in success or failure of a commercial establishment (shop) are location, location and location. What you sell depends on what where you are located. If you sell antique jewelry you better be located in a tony area in the city. Marketing experts have long claimed that location is everything in sales.

James Crail inherited a shoe business. The shop was located at a place which could be called decent but not upmarket. The margins were low but the shop did brisk business. James was lucky to have loyal customers who made sure that they and their family purchased the footwear at Crail's outlet. 'Value for money' is what Crail's father claimed as their strong point.

James was always of the opinion that their business should move to high end products and wanted to stock the latest fashion items. The margins were also high and the clientele rich. He therefore sold all the old stock and purchased costly and fashionable footwear. He also spent on sprucing up the shop.

What do you think happened to his business? The footwear shop was located at a busy intersection but was not known to attract rich clients. The neighborhood was middle class and they stopped visiting his shop as soon as they realized that they no longer stocked daily wear. As a result, James sold hardly anything and the footfalls slowly died away.

What has all this got to do with SEO? Now imagine that your website sells shoes. What kind of links do you think you should attract? Mostly from websites which sell shoes? Or maybe from sites which recommend footwear? In fact Google judges your website by the links you keep. Links become relevant and authoritative if they are associated with you in any manner. This makes lot of sense if you look at it from the traditional perspective. Obviously you are unlikely to be advertising footwear if you were a restaurant. Don't you think a link from a food website to your footwear site is irrelevant and makes no sense?

Backlinks from relevant websites

This is an important lesson – don't run around buying and begging for backlinks from everyone and everybody. Google will discard backlinks from unrelated websites. It doesn't make sense connecting with people who have nothing to do with your business. Instead you should spend your time getting links from authority websites.

If you were a tech site you would like to obtain links from Mashable and TechCrunch not Yahoo Finance or CNBC (unless you are publishing your annual account statement). On the other hand, it will be considered quite prestigious if you could manage backlinks from Huffington Post, Entrepreneur, Inc., Forbes or Wall Street Journal though technically they are not technology sites.

Backlinks from authority sites can easily catapult you to the first page of SERP's, provided you have done your homework on on-page optimization. There are thousands of authority sites. You must explore various possibilities and create as many backlinks as possible from relevant sites.

How does Google identify scrappy sites?

What is a scrappy site anyway? You can easily identify these sites by simply looking at their outbound links. Can a genuine website have a hundred or even fifty outbound links on the home page? You will find no more than five outbound links on genuine website home pages. This is exactly what Google algorithm does – it checks the number of outbound links and you know what happens? Google simply blacklists these sites. It also blacklists those sites which are linked to it. At the very least you will get penalized if your site is found to be friendly with this scrappy site. The lesson is obvious. You should avoid getting backlinks from such scrappy sites.

You can land up in a worse soup if you associate yourself with scrappy sites which link to objectionable sites. No one can help you once you link to sites which have backlinks to porn sites – even gambling sites. The problem here is that scrappy sites link to all kinds of sites. They are kind of democratic when it comes to backlinks. They don't discriminate between porn sites and yours. In real life would you consider befriending someone who is in the porn business? 'Meet my friend. He is a porn agent,' you will introduce your friend to your colleagues.

Mind you there is nothing wrong if you are in the porn business yourself. But in real life people are in rarely in porn business. Google thinks that everyone linked to porn deals in adult stuff and you will be lumped with them.

Thin content is another problem with scrappy sites. You would have noticed that some sites don't have enough content. This is a red flag for Google search algorithm. Google hates sites with thin content which means web pages with less than 200 words. More the content better you will look to Google.

Another misconception about backlinks is about blog comments. People try and get backlinks by commenting on blog posts. When you see a SEO company offer one thousand backlinks for $5, it must immediately raise your radar. This offer will not only not get you results but may also get you blacklisted by Google.

To summarize: Backlinks greater than fifty added to a crazy mix of unrelated and inappropriate backlinks is equal to getting penalized by Google.

Creating content is difficult, especially quality content and Google appreciates this fact. You already know about keywords and the key to great content is to develop content around your keyword.

Great content = Content built around target keyword.

The next step is to promote your content by using off-line SEO strategies. Link building is not a onetime activity. You have to look at your website as a work-in-progress. You are the architect and you have to build your website brick by brick. It takes time and patience to create a masterpiece. When you see a really popular website, with thousands of visitors, you must realize that it must have taken months if not years to reach there.

Consider your website as an investment. Your egg nest takes time and patience to create. You cannot expect results overnight. Billionaire Warren Buffet, the most famous stock investor, repeatedly exhorts investors to think long term. You require a similar strategy in SEO.

Building natural backlinks

Natural backlinks = high authority backlinks

This much everyone can understand. But how do you get natural backlinks? Here again content is the key. Create quality content and other authority sites would like to be friends with you. The challenge here is to build relationships with other website owners. You know by now that obtaining backlinks through commenting on blogs can be dangerous to your website health. A better alternative is to write high quality guest posts for other websites. This gesture will be appreciated and you will be able to get natural backlinks. Another advantage is that Google will look at the content and associate your backlink with it. Referral traffic is another byproduct of writing quality guest posts. Remember that traffic is an important factor in Google ranking.

More traffic means your ranking goes up in search results which means you get even more traffic. This has a compounding effect giving a tremendous boost to your SEO efforts.

Contextual links and bylinks

It is important to know the difference between contextual link and bylink. Contextual link is embedded inside the content. As the name suggests, the link has context which is appreciated more by Google search algorithm. By choosing the right anchor text (you will learn about it later) you will be able to extract maximum link juice from a contextual link. The trick here is not to overdo the contextual part. You should have at most one contextual link inside the guest post.

Bylink, on the other hand is a link which is inserted inside the bio of the author. This bio is attached at the end of a guest post. Of course, bylink is also quite valuable. You should remember to link to your homepage when you are using a bylink.

Try to please your reader, not Google

There is a mistaken belief that search engine optimization means getting Google to rank you higher in search results. In trying to please Google, we sometimes go overboard and use tactics which are actually harmful. Trying to break the google code is not the way to go. Too much analysis will lead you nowhere. Instead you should concentrate on building great content. Google will never have a problem with content. Don't try to bend the rules. SEO does not mean understanding Google search algorithm and trying to break it.

Building great content is the way to go. This does not mean you forget keywords and optimization. You must have a strategy in place which means crafting keywords and building your website content based on these keywords. Your content should attract other websites and must be compelling enough to get backlinks. Each backlink is like an up vote for Google, as long as they are from authority sites which are related.

Focus on content

Creating a content strategy is important. Keywords are important. But when you think about good content everything becomes secondary except the message. Are you providing value to your visitor must be the uppermost question in your mind? Your keyword may have a very low search volume – even five searches a day. It does not matter. Ultimately, the traffic to your site will come from a niche audience ho want to read and hear from you.

You may have read that websites have millions of words of content. People get scared when they hear about such humungous numbers. People try to find shortcuts and this leads them to failure. Instead why not concentrate on writing about something you like, even if you know that the audience is niche.

Google loves data and website owners spend enormous amount of time churning out figures, charts and numbers. Should you be doing this kind of data mining? There are no specific clear-cut answers to such pointed questions.

The fact is that there is no one way to create a great website. You can carry out a small survey and you will realize that websites come in different shapes and dimensions. A hundred page website on shoes, yes shoes, can have an enormous fan following. At the same time a thousand page site on philosophy may attract only few visitors. Which website would you call successful? In fact, the definition of success varies. The website owner on philosophy may be happy with his niche audience. Who knows?

There is another myth on authority sites. People think that authority means something serious and nerdy. People imagine pages of scientific literature written in APA format. The truth is totally different. Authority website may simply mean a site which contains information about a simple solution to a simple problem. Simplicity is sometimes more difficult to achieve. Simplicity requires a different mindset – that of solving real life problems.

The best type of SEO is no SEO at all. Forget that you want to appear on the first page of search results. This focus on search results actually takes you away from success. Simply choose a focus keyword and build your content around it. Give it your best shot. Create the best content ever written on the subject. You know more about the subject you are writing about than anyone else in this world.

Do you have confidence in yourself? Do you love your work? SEO will automatically take care of itself if you take care of your content. The secret of SEO is simple enough. This fact has been written about in many books by many experts but we tend to ignore good advice. You think that there must be something which you are missing. Some kind of secret sauce, perhaps! You will be surprised to know that there is no secret sauce after all. Like the Panda in movie 'Kung Fu Panda' says – There is no secret ingredient.

Create unique, outstanding and personalized content

Why are you reading so much about content when this book is about SEO? This is a good question that requires a detailed answer.

What do you think of when you think of search? Google obviously. Google is synonymous with search. This much we all understand. What most of us don't know is that Google depends on good content for its survival. Google doesn't need anyone or anything. They are above and beyond everything. If you are one of those who are nodding their head there is more news for you. Google depends on content – your content for survival. The day Google does not give appropriate search results, you and everyone will abandon Google search. Maybe you will start Binging – who knows. This is the reason why Google is so particular about what it displays on its search pages. It is quite understandable that Google will love you if you create proper content.

Logic dictates that you produce great content. Logic also says that reworded, hashed up, regurgitated content will not be appreciated by Google. How will Google know that is fresh content and what is copied stuff? Well, this is the secret sauce which Google will not reveal to anyone. If you knew how to make the secret sauce you will game the system and this Google would like to avoid. In the absence of specific knowledge, you are left to deduct some of the ingredients of this secret sauce. What if you come to know that the only ingredient is content?

The relationship between you and Google is symbiotic. This means that you have to help Google which in turn will help you. Your future is linked to the future of Google – no exaggeration.

How do you help Google? Hey, I am too small a guy for this huge task. If you are thinking in this direction, you can quit right now. But you are not too small. Not for Google. If you provide content which is unique and interesting, Google would love to put your website on the first page of search results. What are the ingredients of your secret sauce?

• You provide fresh and unique content which cannot be found on any other website.

• You update content on your website regularly.

• Your competitors copy your content not the other way around.

• Your website content is extensive and thorough.

• Your content and keywords are perfectly matched.

• You are alert and always follow the latest news.

• You grab opportunities by observing weaknesses in competing websites.

Have you wondered why some search results found on the first page of Google are pathetic? They have poor and thin content. The reason is that these web pages are riding piggyback on an authority site. They are enjoying the status of first page because the other pages on the website are doing great in the eyes of Google. Do you think you can turn this situation into a winning opportunity? You can identify such results and create more detailed, elaborate and interesting content revolving around the central keyword. There is a huge opportunity to trump the competition with superior content.

You must have noticed that many web pages which mark their attendance on the first page of search results have scant data. It is apparent they the content is thin and no research has been done on the subject matter. They are there because they are part of an authority site. Here is another great opportunity for you. You can write some very detailed content with plenty of data and research citations and overwhelm the search engine.

Give your content the right context

The internet is filled with uninteresting stuff. The content in some websites is pure trash at the worst or simply stale at best. They lack a soul which is so badly needed. Why can't you substitute this sorry stuff with something with flesh and soul? Mostly the offenders are corporate personalities who are impersonal and insipid as if they were addressing a wall rather than real people. Some big businesses treat their website as the Great Wall of China – it's impressive but no longer useful. Users of such websites are themselves corporate staff and part of official machinery who no longer care about what is happening around them.

This is where you step in. You must create compelling content which hits a person right at the place where it matters – the heart. Personalization of content is not discussed in detail anywhere but it is the most important part of SEO.

The reader must empathize with the content. The reader must feel comfortable. The reader must read and not skip through the text.

What are the factors which personalize content?

- Clear text and clean images

- Text broken into manageable chunks

- Bold and prominent headings which say everything in a few words

- Images which speak a thousand words

- No distractions

If you keep the above factors in mind, the reader will certainly keep you in mind.

Leading the way

Though there is lots of chatter about SEO on the internet, there are very few serious SEO players. SEO specialists at best do a halfhearted job and the website owners know no better. Do you think you can make a difference?

Making a difference is not a choice. It is an imperative. You have to take your SEO role seriously, pullup your sleeves and get on with the hard work. You should go much beyond your competitor. Of course the compensation will be equally rewarding.

You have an advantage over others. You are willing to go the extra yard while others are – well – just doing a job. You don't think it is hard to churn out content every day for years together. Don't get scared, it's not as if you are being given an enormous task. It's quite simple to write content if you put your mind to it. But you have to do more. You have to be innovative and creative all the time. This may be a tougher task but has to be done.

Once you are finished with writing great stuff, you must sit down to write some more great stuff. The beautiful part is that you will start loving the process once you see the results. Continuous first page ranking will put a zing in your life. You will begin to understand the magic of SEO. Nobody can stop you now. You will go and create success like never before.

Originality is the secret to success

Everyone can write. The material available on the internet proves this. It also proves that most of what is written is trash. Original content is appreciated by readers as well as Google. Providing fresh material is a sure shot way to get into the first page of SERP's. So, why don't website owners do it – create fresh and original content. This is because it is difficult. Let's face it. It takes time and patience to be original and that too on a regular basis. At the same time you have tons of content online which can act as an inspiration.

How to eat an elephant?

Now, this is a tough one. Who can eat an elephant? SEO is like eating an elephant. You have to first believe that you can eat an elephant. This belief is the starting point when you pick up the knife and fork. Next, you have to work out an original scheme to complete the task. There are others who have done it. Websites owners have cut through the tough skin and tasted the flesh. They will tell you that it is not easy.

SEO looks like a huge task – more challenging than eating an elephant. The best way to begin is to start from somewhere. Too much of analysis can lead to paralysis. Just pick up a bit and start chewing. You will get a hang of it and the rest would seem easy. The progress you make will make you more enthusiastic. You should be original, creative and think out of the box. After all you don't eat an elephant every day. There is no method to the madness. You must have realized by now that there are no shortcuts. Eating an elephant cannot be done other than to put a part of it in your mouth and chew. You cannot game the system. You and you alone has to eat the whole stuff. It's yours.

So, how do you eat an elephant?

Bit by bit, of course.

The analogy is appropriate because SEO requires digging in every day and doing it bit by bit. You can't do it in one single swoop. You can't eat it whole. SEO is too big and too complex. But once you decide to do it bit by bit you can get to the end for sure.

There are elephants everywhere

True and people are eating them by the truckload. This is an opportunity for you to learn. You can follow the guys who seem to be doing it nicely, with finesse. Original writing does not mean you have to start writing scientific papers. Look around you. Find the best material out there and give it a new twist. Provide fresh perspective to an idea which has been there before and it will become your idea. The best part is that you already know that the idea works. You can go ahead confidently, since you know that you will hit the SEO jackpot.

Ask questions

Ask and you shall receive. The problem is that we don't ask questions, let alone valid ones. If you ask you will certainly get answers. Where do you look for questions and subsequent answers? In your competitor's website. Have you wondered why your competitor's website attracts social sites and bloggers like bees to flowers? Bees get attracted to flowers because the flowers provide nectar. Take out the nectar and the bees will fly away. Clever website owners provide something tangible to social busy bees and bloggers. There is a pot of honey waiting for everyone who participates on their website. Your job is to discover this pot of honey and provide a similar incentive to link with you. Remember that your job is done once you are on the first page of SERP's. You just have to edge out others.

The story of an old stone grinder

Have you seen a stone grinder? Probably not. Stone grinders were used in the old day to grind wheat and other foodstuff. The process was slow and laborious. It took hours to grind a handful of wheat. But the stone grinder never failed. It did not require any fuel or electricity. You had to simply keep grinding away with your hand. In the end you had finely ground wheat, all ready to cook. SEO is like a stone grinder. You put ideas into it and keep churning out quality content. You don't stop till you get finely powdered, high quality content.

SEO, like a stone grinder is all about the process. It is consistency and regularity. There should be some wheat inside the grinder all the time. You can imagine how hard this will be. Grinding away every day can be tedious. It is tough yet it's easy if you love the work. Every time you get weary and disillusioned, remember that there is a pot of gold waiting at the end of the rainbow, just for you.

SEO is not for loners

If you thought that SEO is for lone wolves sitting in the dark shadows and working their spell on the internet, you are wrong. SEO means communication, conversations and building relationships. Google wants quality backlinks to your website. More the merrier. But you just can't get backlinks for free. You have to earn backlinks. How do you do that? You have to constantly communicate with fellow website owners and bloggers. In fact you have to be on first name terms with everyone in the ecosystem. Imagine that you have to build friendships. You just can't walk over to any guy at the bar and shake hands with him. That would be weird. Strangers don't respond to your friendship call unless you get introduced to them. If this is how relationships work in real life, why would you expect the internet to be different?

There are two issues which you must address here. First are your credentials. Is your website or blog worth the relationship you are looking for? You may want to date a movie star but will the star reciprocate? You need good content to attract friends and well-wishers. The second issue is reciprocity. How can you help fellow bloggers and website owners reach their goal?

Never think that helping others means giving from your plate. More you give more will be available to you. This is the beauty of sharing.

There are many ways to be of help. You can write a great post for others. You can comment intelligently on the posts of others. You can mention their name in your articles. The list of giving is endless. But what do you see in actual life? You receive a cold email from a stranger who wants a backlink urgently. No introduction, nothing. How are you likely to respond? Ignore the request and move on. Do not expect any favors unless you are ready to give favors.

Making friends the traditional way

There used to be a time when people used to exchange letters. Letters have been replaced by emails. They are faster and more efficient means of communication. Email lists are something which you will have to work on if you wish to succeed in the SEO world. This is the only way to reach out to others and let them know what you are up to. Newsletters can be easily delivered to the inbox of all the likeminded friends and acquaintances with minutes of you publishing an article on your website. Obviously, you have to write outstanding content if you want others to get hooked. Make sure that you respond enthusiastically when you get mail from others. Reciprocity is the common link between you and others. You may think that it's a waste of time commenting on other posts. It's normal. Human beings are selfish creatures. But you can't afford to be selfish. Think of it as community service.

What happens when you have a mailing list? Your website or blog receives a blast of visitors. Your article is discussed in social media and widely circulated. Many sites link to your article creating valuable link juice. Google notices the unusual activity and drinks the aroma of effective SEO. It pushes your site to the top of SERPs. Okay, this is an ideal outcome. But you will create a small ripple on the internet.

Remember that email marketing is a part of SEO which is outside the control of Google. Your site cannot get penalized because you sent too many emails. Avoid sending junk mails and you can enjoy the benefits of email marketing forever.

Promoting your content

Email is not the only way you can promote your content. We will discuss various ways to promote content in the next chapter. Here we will briefly touch upon it. Promotion is like winking, you have to be seen to be winking. You have to wink in broad daylight. You can't wink in the dark and expect others to notice.

You must acquire the habit of guest posting if you want to promote yourself. Guest posting is like giving away your valuables free of cost. Why would do that? You spend hour's fine tuning your articles and posts, use keywords judiciously, make it readable and then give it away. This does not make sense. Once again think of it as the cost of social acceptance. Other website owners and bloggers would appreciate your large hearted gesture and reciprocate by gifting a backlink to you. They may even mention you in their social network. What do you think will happen? You will get traffic from sources to which you did not have access earlier. These are valuable connections which cannot be bought by paying money. Your network can only spread through sharing of content. Large corporate salivate at the prospect of getting their content shared on social media. They even give gifts and prices for sharing content. They do this because they know the value of shared content.

What does a backlink look like?

You have read so much about backlinks that they are surely coming out of your ears by now.

If backlinks re coming out of your ears, it is not necessarily a bad thing because they are a critical component of SEO. So, what does a backlink look like? Backlinks are actually text which contains the link to the website which it refers to. This text is called Anchor text. It's like holding a ship to the ground. The backlink rests on an anchor text. The reader sees the anchor text and not the link. You can see the link if you hover your mouse over the anchor text. Let's examine a hyperlink and the anchor text:

<a href= "http://www.johnshoes.com "> Quality shoes </a>

Here, http://www.johnshoes.com is the website and 'Quality shoes' is the anchor text. You will see only 'Quality shoes' on the website while clicking on it will take you to the website http://www.johnshoes.com.

Why do you need anchor text?

As mentioned earlier, backlinks are an important part of SEO. Google considers each link as an upvote for your website. The backlinks are supported by anchor text. In the above examples, you can see that 'Quality shoes' is the anchor text. The reader has no problem associating this anchor text with the website it is linked to. You are sure that if you click on this link you will reach a website on quality shoes.

Clearly, you have to associate your anchor text with the activity on your website. If your keyword is also 'Quality shoes' Google algorithm, which decides your search ranking, will know for sure that you have done a good job.

Now consider this:

The website containing the backlink has nothing to do with the stuff you are promoting on your website. Looks suspicious isn't it? Why would a website on granite and marble products carry a link to shoes? Google algorithm quickly comes to the conclusion that this is a useless link inserted to fool the search engine. As a result, even if you worked hard to earn a backlink, google will discard it as unrelated.

The lesson is clear. Not all backlinks are made equal. Don't waste your time, money and effort in getting backlinks from unrelated sites.

Now consider this:

The website on granite and marble products also links to many porn sites. This means you are living in a bad neighborhood. Google, in this case may decide to penalize you for this activity. It's dangerous to associate your website with toxic sites. Google algorithm is intelligent but not human. It looks at the context and decides to label it as a quality link or otherwise. It has only two basic indicators – link and anchor text. Of course it has the originating website and the destination website.

Once Google search algorithm finds a suitable anchor text and the link, it crawls through the destination website. This is to make sure that the anchor text is related to the destination website. It examines the anchor text in relation to the content on the designation web page. It provides a certain value to the backlink based on all these factors.

You should therefore make sure that your anchor text and content on the destination match. This creates the necessary relevance and adds weight to the backlink.

The relevance of anchor text in SEO

Can toxic links lead to blacklisting of your website?

Can backlinks with appropriate anchor text from authority sites boost your search ranking?

Can this knowledge be used by competitors to get other sites blacklisted by Google?

Can they intentionally add a backlink from a porn site to yours and then stand back to watch the fun?

Can you get banned for backlinks from inappropriate sites?

Banning is an extreme step and it is unlikely that your website will get blacklisted due to seeding backlinks in inappropriate sites. Experienced SEO experts are of the opinion that Google would not give you any credit for the backlink. But bad neighborhood has negative consequences, in the sense that your website would be seen with jaundiced eyes.

What about buying text links from suspicious websites? Will this get you banned? Let's assume that your competitor buys links in a bad neighborhood like a casino site and a   couple of porn sites. These links lead to your site. What do think will be the consequences? Will google ban you now? Obviously, if banning was so easy, all your competitor has to do is pay a couple of dollars and get you banned. Google will not buy this logic since every site will get banned eventually.

Looking into anchor text

Should you use the same anchor text in all the backlinks?

Website owners are tempted to overdo their keyword-anchor text combination to the extent that the links look artificial. This may impact your overall SERP's. One trick which is used by website owners and SEO experts is to use a totally different anchor text from the natural one they use regularly. You can do this twice for every ten anchor texts.

Should you link to the home page or different pages?

Another important factor to be considered is the actual link to the website. You should try and add different anchor texts which lead to different web pages. This is an excellent way to get focused audience as well as distribute link juice all over the site.

This spreading of links across the website sends an important message to Google: that your website is extensive and is providing important information. This boosts your search ranking and you start figuring in the first page of search results.

Cascading effect

Once your website starts appearing on the first page of Google search results you will see an enormous jump in traffic. This will in turn improve your ranking further because traffic is something Google looks at closely. In fact, authority sites manage to remain on top of search results because of their traffic.

What should you do once you start attracting visitors? Wouldn't it be a pity if you do all the hard work only to see visitors leaving your site without spending time to explore the goodies? There is a lot which can be done to make visitors stick around your site. This is where your content plays major role in creating stickiness – ability to keep visitors glued to your website. We will learn about these and other issues in the coming chapters.

Chapter 4 - Analyzing your website

Have you heard about the story of an elephant and five blind men? Once upon a time there were five blind men. They had heard about an enormous animal called an elephant and wanted to know more about it. One fine day they set out to the zoo and requested the zoo keeper to allow them to touch an elephant. Fortunately, the zoo had a tame elephant which allowed people to touch and feel it without protesting.

One by one the blind men touched the elephant. The first blind man caught hold of the tail and announced that an elephant looked like a rope. The next blind man happened to touch the body and was sure that an elephant looked like a huge wall. The third imagined the elephant to look like a tube, the fourth like a canine tooth and fifth declared that an elephant was exactly like the trunk of a tree. Each blind man was right in his place but was wrong in actual fact. They did not get the whole picture but based their opinion on partial information. Are you assessing your website like the blind men?

Okay, now that you have optimized your site and got the best backlinks, what do you do? Wait for the traffic to pour in and buy your stuff? Are you assessing the value of your SEO effort or simply keeping your fingers crossed? You will only get the whole picture if you understand what the whole picture is all about. The ultimate purpose of a website is monetization, not SEO. The ultimate test is whether you make money from your website. You have to analyze your website from this perspective.

Measuring and evaluating the success or failure of your SEO effort is important. By doing this you will know what works and what doesn't. You have to keep changing your tactics and align yourself with the trend. What is the point if you attract huge traffic but no one buys from your website? To understand the dynamics of your website, you must watch the trends and developments carefully. You must gather insight into the user experience. You must measure the impact your SEO has on the bottom line.

With this in mind let's look more closely at your website.

1.   What is the amount of traffic you are getting from organic search? This is a verifiable test and cannot be manipulated or misunderstood. More the traffic more successful is your SEO strategy.

2.   The second aspect is how to increase organic traffic? Can you play with the keywords? Which keywords are fetching you maximum traffic? Reining your SEO strategy is a continuous process and there is no end to refinement.

3.   Your competitor is your best friend when it comes to comparison. You must know your competitors website better than you know about your own. Drill deep into the competitor's content. How is the home page different from yours? Look at all the elements – from images,

color scheme, font size and the actual content. You need not blindly copy all the elements. In fact you should not copy all the elements but pick and choose judiciously. You can even learn from mistakes made by your competitor. Next, look at the category pages. Do they focus on a single keyword or long-tail-keywords? Which long tail keywords do they use? Are they appropriate for you? By doing this you can cut down on lots of research and time which you would otherwise spend on identifying keywords.

4.   It has been seen that websites which have a strong brand name get organic traffic from these keywords. Traditional businesses spend an enormous amount of time and money building brands. They carry the brand value to their online activities as well. Chances are that you are not a branded company and therefore you have to depend on generic keywords to attract organic traffic. This can be a challenge. This is one reason cited by SEO experts why you must sell niche products which have intrinsic value. The

downside of a niche market is the consumer base which is limited compared to generic products. You have to find a median solution to extract the most out of your SEO efforts

5.   Single keywords usually attract more traffic than long tailed keywords. Focusing on a single keyword is anyway not advisable since you want search engines not to discount your content due to obvious optimization effort. Long tail keywords, on the other hand, get low traffic. People are lazy and use a single keyword for searches. But you must remember that steel does not exist in real life – only iron ore. Long tail keywords are like iron ore. They have the inherent quality to transform into steel. You should construct several long tail keywords which you should distribute among different web pages. Never delete a web page just because the long tail keywords do not work. Add additional pages to accommodate new keywords. Google and other search engines will treat you with

respect if you have more web pages and offer better content than your competitor.

6. You don't have to beat the search engine algorithm. You only have to beat your competitor. Many website owners think that search engine is their enemy who they have to conquer. They spend inordinate amount of time trying to crack the Google algorithm. This is a futile exercise. Treat the search engine as a friend trying to help you fetch traffic. You only have to be a notch better than your competitor to hog all the traffic. As such, the online market is immense and there is enough for everyone.

7. For some unknown reason, website owners focus on the home page for SEO. This is not a good strategy. It is better to target specific pages with one specific keyword. It is obvious that the effort required to target several keywords is tough. Did you think SEO is easy? When you have many keywords, you have to develop that many inbound links for each of them. For example, if you have twenty keywords,

you will require at least one thousand inbound links. This looks huge and impossible. The secret is to spread the effort over several months. Also you should remember that the inbound links should be from authority sites – not any website. You should avoid toxic neighborhoods and get any links removed from such sites.

8.   The home page is not an ideal target page for inbound links due to another reason. People who click on such links land on the home page from where they have to once again start their search for the right page. This is frustrating and many visitors may abandon their search right there. To avoid such a situation, it is better to target inner pages which are directly related to the anchor text.

9.   When a visitor to your site abandons it without clicking on any other page, it means that they have found nothing worthwhile on your website. This is also called bounce rate. Google search algorithm takes bounce rate into consideration when calculating the value or

worth of your website. Many site owners, especially those who do their own SEO, do not care less for bounce rate and Google in turn does not care for them. Merely getting people to visit your site through organic search does not make you popular. You require stickiness from visitors if you want Google to respect you. This can only be done by making your site more attractive. You should provide an excellent experience for your customers if you want them to stick around. Increase the appeal to visitors by providing better content than your competitors. An increase in bounce rate should be treated as a warning sign by you. Take corrective action before you move ahead with your SEO effort.

10.   Another useful indicator which you must track is the new versus returning visitor. What happens in a traditional business environment? Customers who are happy with the service become loyal and visit your office more often. It's the same for a website. Visitors who get the right information which they are seeking tend to come

back for more. These visitors bookmark your site for easy access. When you see returning visitors it means your site is effective. On the other hand you cannot lose sight of new visitors. You need a healthy diet of new people who will become your loyal customers. How else will you get an opportunity to impress them

Consider the two issues separately –

•	High Bounce rate means you have to improve the quality of your website

•	Low new visitor count means you have to improve SEO.

11.	There is another task which you must undertake. In case of a bounced visitor, you should identify the keyword and landing page of that visitor. This will give you a fair idea where you may be going wrong. Maybe the landing page is not appropriate. Maybe there is a mismatch between keyword/anchor text and land page. This type of in-depth study requires time and effort which is unavoidable if you want your SEO effort to be rewarded.

Chapter 5 - Promoting your website

Now that you've a website that is optimized and ready to be showcased to the world, start promoting your website through social media. There are various methods to promote your website online to improve search ranking and appear on the first page of search. Here are some methods you can use to promote your website.

1. Social Networking Sites

Nowadays everybody is on social media. Be it Facebook, Twitter, WhatsApp or Instagram or Snapchat, Google Plus, LinkedIn; you name it and millions of people are on it. Since it is free to have an account anybody and everybody has a social media account. In other words a social media profile acts as your online reputation management page. These sites allow you to connect and network with friends and likeminded people. At the same time you can also promote and advertise your business to the world.

There are umpteen ways to promote your website/ business. You can 'tag' people so that you make sure that your product gets a wider audience. Facebook and Instagram also offer paid advertising. You can promote for free or through paid advertising. Make more than 5000 friends and your advertisement will go viral within a few minutes. You can also target your marketing efforts to a specific geographical area. Geo targeted marketing will help to popularize your business in your neighborhood area. For example – if you're running a restaurant in Dallas, you would only like to advertise in the local area and not in New York. At the same time if your product can be used worldwide like apparels, then you may need to advertise worldwide.

Social media has changed the way people do business. Sarah made a website for swimsuits and started promoting it through social media. Her website was interactive where people could submit their measurements for perfect swimwear. She used SEO tactics to name her website so that she gets ranked high on search. Initially she used the local postal service to send parcels to clients but later moved to mailing them all over the country. What started as a hobby in her basement turned into a lucrative business within two years. Today Sarah not only sells through her website but also uses other market places like Amazon and EBay to sell her products.

There are many success stories like this on social media marketing. All you need is zest and zeal combined with passion to make it big in this beautiful world.

2. **Blogging**

Blogging is the best way to make yourself heard. If you're into marketing your business then creating a blog along with your website will help you to keep visitors returning to your website. Updating your blog on a regular basis will help the search crawler to visit your website often.

This will automatically improve your ranking on the search engine.

Ideally your blog should contain info graphics, how to tutorials, videos, interesting pictures about your business, etc. Be clear and concise while writing a blog post. In case you're not good at writing hire ghostwriters and content management experts to do the job. Your content needs to be unique and should contain keywords that pertain to your niche.

Use topical incidents and link them to your niche to create a post. This will help your blog to appear high on the search results. For example- When Steve Jobs passed away Google crashed for an hour or so as millions of people around the world were looking for information about him. Use Google Analytics to find out the highest searched keywords in your niche and infuse them into your blog post.

Say you're selling pet food and your blog is about pets then you can include a post on Donald trump's pet or Barack Obama's pet as their names are widely searched online. Be creative and innovative. Blog posts are the best way to get connected with your audience.

3. **Blog Marketing**

Visit your competitors or other people in your niche blogs and post comments on their post. That'll enable you to add your blog/ website link in the comments section. These links are crawled by search engines that in turn help to improve you in search results. These blogs are commonly known as 'do follow' blogs.

4. **Forum Marketing**

There are social forums related to your niche where you can your community people and communicate with them. Replying to questions on forums will help you to connect with people. This will build your reputation as an expert in your niche. Use forums that allow 'do follow' links so that you can leave your website link in the answer section.

5. Search Engine Submission

This is a very important step to get you seen online. Submit your website to the most popular search engines like Google, Yahoo, Bing, etc. By submitting your website Google will start visiting your site to see the activity occurring there. Constant updating of your blog will help you to move higher on search.

6. Directory Submission

It is believed that directory submission is no longer valid. But that is not so. Submitting articles to various niche directories can still enable you to get back links. It may not instantly improve your search rank but can add to link building.

7. Social Bookmarking

Having icons of social sites like Stumble Upon, Reddit, Delicious and Digg instantly broadcasts your website to millions of people around the world. These bookmarkers are search engine favorites as they're constantly updated. Be careful while using 'tags' as they help to broadcast your site. This is sure to increase traffic.

8. Link Baiting

You can always link your blog post to another blog in your niche and give credits to that blog on your blog. This will aid in link popularity.

9. Photo Sharing

In case you've niche pictures on your blog about your product upload it to photo sharing sites like Picasa, Pixabay, Stocksnap, etc. Leave your link there. By allowing people to share your pictures they'll give 'picture courtesy' link to your website. This will attract traffic to your site too.

10. Video Marketing

YouTube is one of the widely watched video sites online. Just like you share pictures share videos about your product on YouTube. Copy the link to your YouTube Channel and put it on all the other social media platforms like Facebook, Twitter, Instagram, etc. this will get you more audience.

11. **Business Reviews**

RateitAll, Shvoong, Kaboodle, Stylefeeder are business review sites where you can ask your friends to write review about your business. Have a few reviews so that people know that you're genuine.

12. **Local Listings**

There are local listings like Google listing, Yahoo Local, etc that offer listing your website to your local neighborhood. Say your product is related to local consumption then it is wise to advertise locally and not compete in the global market. This will help you to reach your target audience.

13. **Article Submission**

Article submission used to be effective till a few years ago for link building and improving search engine ranking. But nowadays Google has downgraded their importance. Still submitting to article directories like ezine, go articles can help you to gain a few links.

14. **Sell on e-commerce sites**

If your product is for consumers then besides having your own website to sell, you can also post the items on e-commerce sites like Amazon.com. This will help in sales of your product instantly as Amazon sells at least 10 products per second. It is one of the largest e-commerce sites in the world.

Chapter 6 - Using social media as enablers

There used to be a time when SEO and social media marketing were different branches of online marketing. We have now reached a stage when you can't separate one from the other. They are in fact complimentary strategies. Today, SEO and social media marketing are interlinked to an extent that they have combined together to form a single inbound marketing tool.

The appeal of social media marketing is immediate and powerful. The reach of social media sites like Facebook is immense. They can bring huge inorganic traffic to your doorstep and the effort required is much less that for pure play SEO. This is not to suggest that you stop SEO efforts altogether. Social media marketing and SEO must go hand in hand to promote your website. The most beautiful part is that your SEO effort can boost your social media presence and social media marketing may improve your search ranking. It is a symbiotic relationship in which both parties prosper. It doesn't take a rocket scientist to understand the dynamic interplay of SEO and social media. Leaving aside the praise heaped on the mutual benefit of these two approaches to online marketing, you would be wondering how to connect the dots between the two. What are the strategies you must adopt to derive maximum benefit? Let's examine the nits and bolts of this mutually inclusive strategy.

1. Following the followers

There can be no denying that the number of followers is the new metrics of success – both personal and business. Individuals boast of millions of Twitter followers. Businesses keep in touch with their customers through 140 characters. There is no need for more characters. A tiny little Tweet from Donald trump, the president of America, can create an earthquake. The power of Twitter cannot be underestimated. Surprisingly followers and connections are simply not capitalized by businesses. One reason is that SEO experts don't know how to connect the dots or they are simply not interested. This is detrimental to your website and overall SEO effort.

Your social media followers can improve traffic to your website tremendously. When a person visits your site through organic search, he or she does not influence anyone else to do so. When a person follows you via a Facebook page, he or she has the power to influence a hundred others to visit your site. The cascading effect is so powerful that it brushes aside any SEO effort. The inherent potential to multiply your traffic is huge.

Unfortunately, the process of growing a customer base through social media marketing is slow. Winning followers is a slog. There are thousands of others vying for attention. The distractions are too many. Social media is full of butterflies that flit from one flower to another without any sense of logic or purpose. There is total chaos out there and you are likely to lose focus in such an environment. The only solution is to be patient and develop relationships than merely soliciting traffic. Of course, a small spark can set your efforts on fire. A single post can elevate you to a higher place. But it is better to build a steady fire and wait for the results.

You should have conversations with your followers than advice. You should ask for information, solicit feedback and look for opportunities to help the friends. You cannot just believe the power of appreciation till you receive a flood of positive feedback. Share ideas; don't thrust your ideas on Facebook friends. Seek feedback, not impose yourself. Don't be judgmental. Be polite and respect the privacy of others. Conversations will turn into traffic for your website bit this will take time.

2.   Have you forgotten the good old backlinks? Social media engagements don't only mean having a conversation; they give you an opportunity to see perfectly legitimate backlinks. Google, as you know by now, loves backlinks

from multiple sources. This gives you a humungous opportunity and opens up new avenues for you. You can share the latest posts or articles with your Twitter friends by a mere click of your mouse. Some plugins in WordPress can automatically send tweets once you have posted on your site. Make sure that the Twitter, Facebook or any other social media connections get to read something worthwhile on your site. Get them hooked to your content and your search ranking will soar to unimaginable heights.

Weaving your conversation into older threads and conversations is an art which you must master. The entire operation or exercise is wholly dependent on the quality of your content. In effect, you can seed backlinks into your feed and solicit more conversation. You should allow the social media conversation to branch and spread. As described previously, this can have a cascading or multiplying effect.

3.   Some call it bait. Some call it persuading. Some call it compelling. Whatever may be the

terminology, social media marketing means attracting attention. You may have the greatest content but unless you attract eyeballs, your effort will go unnoticed. Your content on social media must look like an advertisement. Your caption must entice, seduce and grab the attention of readers. Remember that you are now competing against a whole lot of audience – amateurs, professionals, housewives, college students, teens ....Everyone is a writer in his own way. A family photograph with a cute little baby can attract more 'likes' than your insipid post on 'shoes'. Your endeavor has to make your shoes look more romantic and desirable. It's difficult and if you are wondering about its feasibility you are dead on target. But you have to find a way out. What about this: "Paris Hilton wears stunning stilettos to Oscars. Designed by El Domingo from the famous Italian school of fashion, the pair was specially created for Paris Hilton. Read more........"

It's you job to make the routine look like the sublime. It can be done. It has been done. Just put in a little more effort.

4.   Have you noticed that whenever you search for a particular keyword, social media sites turn up first on the search results, especially when the keyword is a trending subject? Google loves updates and news. It wants to display news while it happens. Connecting the dots does not take a genius. Look out for the latest trends and cover the news on your website. Spread the news through your social media channels and wait for the traffic to gush in. Google trends is a good place to look for the latest happenings. You should take care that the anchor text you use in social media is appropriate and is linked to the right web page. You can quickly master this strategy once you get a hang of it. Readers are more likely to click on your link if you offer the latest news. Including graphics is an excellent way to get attention.

5.   Pay attention to the title, anchor text and overall impact of your post. Add a video or infographic if you have the time. This will grab the attention of users. Every comment and like is an up vote for Google. If someone shares your post, you are likely to get many more hits and this will improve your domain authority. Retweets have the power to kindle a major fire. Every little bit improves your authority. What this means is that your website goes up in SERP's. This in turn results in organic traffic to your site. This is a win-win situation for you.

6.   Participation in local events is a great way to get into the first page of search results. Every event must be celebrated on your social media channel. This is a huge opportunity especially if you are into a local market. For example, a restaurant can easily conduct competitions and events which can be shared through Facebook. Instant discounts can be announced through tweets which can become viral. Google

encourages news on local events and this gives you a terrific break to get into organic search.

7.   Social media marketing is increasingly being used for brand and reputation building. You can showcase your brand on various social media channels without damaging your finances. A lesser known brand can get a boost in search ranking if seriously promoted on social media. Google search algorithm will give you an extra point for each mention on social media. This will get reflected in search results for your brand name.

In the end what matters is user experience. Social media marketing is more about communication and sharing. If you have quality content to share, your social media friends will flock to your site. This will, in turn, improve your popularity and traffic. Google, as you know, loves traffic and it will work overtime to present you in organic search result pages.

If by chance you are thinking to bypass social media marketing, you must rethink your strategy. Social media has the power to single handedly boost your presence on the internet.

Chapter 7 - SEO for WordPress

WordPress is unarguably the most popular CMS used by millions of individuals and companies. It is therefore appropriate to discuss SEO for WordPress in a separate chapter.

Why use WordPress in the first place? It's easy to use and even novices can jumpstart their online activities without much fuss. You don't have to know html (Hypertext Markup Language). In fact you need not know anything about software. Everything can easily be set up with the help of WordPress CMS or Content management System. There is a reason why it's not called software. Well, the simple answer is that it isn't software. It's a powerful tool for creating and presenting online content. SEO for WordPress is an important part of the process, which involves many plugins. Sometimes you can get carried away by the simplicity of WordPress and ignore the SEO aspect altogether which is a huge blunder. Your future growth and search engine ranking can get negatively impacted if you don't pay attention to the SEO aspects related to WordPress. Let's have a look at the basic structure of WordPress to understand how you can extract the best out of it from SEO perspective.

Is WordPress optimized for search engines?

When you have such a fantastic tool like WordPress, there is a tendency to attach mythical and grandiose qualities with it. People who are in the business of WordPress market the tool as if clients need not do anything but can reap extraordinary benefits from adopting WordPress. Of course, the clients are made to pay through their nose before they can sit back and enjoy the free lunch. Unfortunately there is nothing called a free lunch.

WordPress can be said to be SEO friendly which is quite different from SEO optimized. WordPress is SEO ready but not optimized. Therefore read carefully when someone is pitching WordPress to you. What are the exact words? Friendly or optimized?

WordPress hosting

There are many popular hosting firms which offer WordPress hosting. You can choose a cheap host if you are limited by monetary resources. However, you should check whether the hosting provider has a control panel to install WordPress and other associated tools like plugins and widgets.

Some hosting service providers also offer managed WordPress hosting which means there will be someone to help you install and maintain your website. As such, you may go managed WordPress hosting if you have deep pockets. Even otherwise it's not difficult to handle WordPress on your own.

WordPress Themes

WordPress is built around themes. You have to setup a theme over your WordPress installation. Makes sure that you have the latest version of

WordPress and the theme works with the current version. WordPress upgrades versions constantly in response to various vulnerabilities and threats.

You can choose between a free WordPress theme and a paid one. There are thousands of free themes which are quite good but if you are planning a heavy duty site, you might as well go for a more robust paid theme with extensive features. From the SEO perspective some free themes may not be suitable. Look for the following issues before installing a theme.

1.   There is nothing called a free lunch. When a provider gives away something free they want something in return. Usually, a free theme will come with a few strings attached. The most common is a link back to the theme provider. Make sure that you get rid of the link or this may negatively impact your SEO efforts.

2.   Another factor which you must keep in mind when choosing a free theme is whether you will get an upgrade version later which is

compatible with the latest version of WordPress. Your site may become a sitting duck to security threats if you don't upgrade themes regularly. Security breaches generally occur through vulnerabilities in themes.

3.   It is a good practice if you first read reviews and feedback on the theme you plan to install. Themes which take a long time to load should be avoided since this will hamper your SEOP effort. Themes must be mobile compatible since many visitors to your site would drop in and browse from their mobiles. You don't want to miss the customers who are addicted to their mobile.

4.   Make sure that the theme is a one click install. You don't want to go through a torturous route to WordPress.

Page and Post in WordPress

Now that you have successfully installed a theme, you will be able to add content. You can either choose to add a page or post to your website. This is not the right place to discuss the details, which can get from any WordPress book. There are some issues which you must in mind when using WordPress. Choose only one category when adding a post. Google may assume that you have added duplicate content if you post simultaneously to multiple categories. Moreover, visitors to your site would not be confused when they see a post under different categories.

What should you do to optimize a WordPress site?

Remember that this book is about SEO and not WordPress. How do you optimize a WordPress site? Though WordPress does not come in a box which is full optimized, it is certainly SEO friendly. There are several plugins which can convert your WordPress site into a mean SEO machine.

The foundation of SEO is content and keywords are the brick and mortar on which this foundation is erected. Content and keywords go together in creating a super-efficient and optimized website. In the end, what matters is SERPs and conversion. The first step therefore is to choose a good SEO plugin.

All In One SEO Pack is installed in thousands of WordPress sites and can be installed without batting an eyelid. Similar is the case with WordPress SEO by Yoast. In addition there are tens of free SEO plugins which could be equally effective but do your due diligence before choosing them. Your chosen SEO plugin must be compatible with WordPress and compliant with all the requirements. How about future upgrading? Sometimes you see a fantastic plugin designed by an unknown entity and you choose to use it. You realize after some time that the plugin developer has vanished and the installation is no longer compatible with the version of WordPress you are currently using. This scenario is played often because developing plugins is a not too complex a task and many individual developers do it for fun. Many come up with brilliant SEO plugins but vanish when they get tired of the novelty of creating a product. Support for the plugin also takes a toss when you don't know whom to approach when there is a problem. A good plugin must have a suitable public support forum in case of need.

Remember that a SEO plugin is only as good as the user. You still have to come up with suitable keywords. You still have to produce quality content. A WordPress plugin is not going to do this for you.

If you recall, we discussed about developing relationships and having conversations to create a proper SEO environment. This also goes for a WordPress site. Modern WordPress themes allow you to add social interaction to your onsite activities. There are many social plugins which automate the task of social media engagement. BuddyPress is an excellent social media plugin. Enrich user experience by adding a plugin which encourages social media interaction. Allow your audience to create their own content. Let the visitors participate and interact through forums. These activities will keep your website abuzz and add value to your SEO effort.

Here are some plugin you should be interested in.

All In One SEO WordPress Plugin

All In One SEO WordPress Plugin is a great WordPress SEO plugin and perhaps the most popular. There are two versions – Free and pro. For most users, the free plugin would do nicely. The pro version is for very large WordPress installations and ecommerce sites.

This plugin is for SEO novices who hardly know anything about optimization and couldn't care less. This plugin automates many SEO functions including optimization of the Title tag. Google attaches value to alt tags to images and this task is efficiently carried out by All In One SEO WordPress Plugin.

This plugin has many advanced features which you can use as you progress through different stages of SEO.

WordPress SEO by Yoast

WordPress SEO by Yoast is a competitor to All In One SEO WordPress Plugin. It has very high rating among SEO plugins and treated with respect. You would be surprised to know that some of the established and high traffic websites use WordPress SEO by Yoast. It also automates many SEO activities like keyword density checker. It provides a rating based on your onsite and offsite SEO activities.

SEOPressor

This plugin is another popular SEO tool used extensively by WordPress users. It has a keyword tool which enables you to discover keywords which are long tailed, from the content on the page or post. SEOPressor WordPress plugin is a good alternative to keyword research tool. You save time in optimizing your page or post content by using this plugin. It also has many social integration features which are very useful.

SEO Cleaner

WordPress is an excellent content management system, no doubt, but it also has some inherent problems. It generates lots of junk along with relevant html code. This junk can considerably slow down page loading which Google takes it as a weakness. SEO Cleaner WordPress Plugin is used to clean up the content on the pages and posts which are generated automatically. This speeds up the overall performance of the website and makes it dearer to Google search algorithm. Moreover, let's not forget the user. Fast page load means users will not abandon your site and you need not worry about visitors abandoning your site.

SEO Friendly Images Pro

SEO does not mean keywords alone. There are many aspects which are related to SEO. You may already know that though Google search algorithm is smart, it still can't read images. Instead it relies on alternative tags to identify an image. Many WordPress users either forget or ignore to tag the images due to time constraints or just plain laziness. SEO Friendly Images Pro comes to the rescue of the couch potatoes. It automates the function of adding title and alternative tag or alt tag to all images. It saves a lot of time and effort of the website owner.

SEO Friendly Images Pro has a powerful feature which allows your website to load faster. Since images are a major culprit resulting in slow web page loading, this plugin circumvents this issue by loading images only when they are in sight on the web page.

SEO Friendly Images

This is another plugin to add alt text and title to your images automatically. Don't forget to use this plugin since you will certainly get traffic from Google image search from it.

Ultimate Video SEO Plugin

With the advent of faster internet connections, videos are increasingly used on websites. Like images, Google algorithm cannot understand video content. Ultimate Video SEO Plugin is a wonderful addition to your WordPress plugins. This plugin automatically generates thumbnails on the search results pages. Imagine how useful this plugin can be for video heavy sites?

Generally, website owners use a link to the video source from which the video is fetched. For example, YouTube is used to store videos which are fetched when it is requested by a website. Ultimate Video SEO Plugin can fetch details directly from hosting services like YouTube. Ultimately your videos land up higher in search engine results pages which in turn drives more traffic to your website. The developer of this plugin has stopped working on future versions. Therefore you must exercise caution when using this plugin.

WP Social SEO Booster

Social is in like never before. People are using Facebook and Twitter as never before. Even Donald Trump, President of United States uses Twitter to announce major policy initiatives. Only the ignorant will bypass the power of social media. WP Social SEO Booster allows you automate many social media tasks.

Google Sitemap

Google bot crawls through you website. This bot is called the crawler due to obvious reasons. Sometimes it can get confused and take the wrong turn. To keep it crawling through all the web pages in an organized manner you require a sitemap. With Google Sitemap plugin you can automatically create a sitemap and even submit it to the Google webmaster tool.

Chapter 8 - SEO through a lens

We have gone through the entire gamut of SEO activities and you can rest now. Can you? Here comes the boring yet the most important task. You have to go through every little SEO activity with a toothcomb.

Let's view our website from a distance. How does it look to you? Does it look like a professional job? First impressions are everything. Look at the color scheme, font size, images and rest of the feely and touchy stuff. Is our website attractive?

Oh yes, of course. Good. Let's move ahead. Now look at the title tag with a lens. The title of your page can make or break the SEO ranking. The Google crawler looks at the Title first and forms its own first impression. Pay attention to the keyword. Is it right at the beginning of the title? If not, can you move the keyword to the front? Keep your brand in front of the title tag. If your brand is unknown, you will get any joy by using it as keyword. This is a mistake which everyone makes. Leave the brand name to big brands. Instead you should focus on the usability of the keyword.

Once you are done with the home page, which is the most crucial part of your website, you can now pay attention to the category pages. Think as if you are the Google crawler (without the sting). How do your category pages look like? Optimize each page and post, one by one. The Title, keywords, meta and everything. Take your time. The maximum amount of link juice is out here – in the category pages. Make sure that you squeeze maximum from the pages. Look at the content. Is it relevant to the keyword and Title? Users get terribly disappointed if the title and content do not match. The content must make users and search engine happy. The content should be rich and complimented by suitable images. Don't think you can fool anyone (Google or user) by providing thin content. Each page or post must have at least 500 words of content. Can be more but never less.

Let's now look at the links on each page. Ideally you should not have more than one link for every hundred words of content. If you have 500 words, you can have at most five outbound links (links within the website are not included). Google search engine can get vexed if it notices unnecessary outbound links. This will raise a red flag. Be careful. People are usually greedy and add as many outbound links because they get paid for it. Avoid the temptation. Do not carry too many Google ads when you join AdSense program. They distract and annoy the user. Avoid advertisements on your website altogether if possible.

Images can tell a story better than a thousand words

Text can be boring and large amount of uninterrupted text can drive away the most academic visitor. You must intersperse your text with relevant images. These images should not divert from the main theme of the web page. Images of nudes may look good but are a distraction. Avoid getting sentimental and romantic. There is place for such things but not here on your website. Images should be appropriate and should be optimized for SEO. This means you should use a proper title and alt tag.

Images must satisfy both the user and search engine. Use proper color scheme for images. Avoid bold and jarring colors even though you are tempted by it.

Links once again

You have to spend an equal amount of time looking at your external links. Have a close look at your anchor texts. The complexity of anchor texts lies in the fact that it should fit on the page in which it is carried. This means there should be coherence between the content of the page and anchor text. Next the link to the anchor text should take the user to a page on your website which contains relevant content. Otherwise the user, though clicking on the anchor text, will abandon yours site.

You should examine the website in which you have placed your anchor text. Does it happen to reside in a bad neighborhood? If so, all your efforts in getting better ranking will go for a toss. There should be no link to a porn site or a gambling site on the website from which you are getting the backlink. Google does not like porn and gambling sites. Google likes a clean image and does not associate with shady people. If you want to be friends with Google you should avoid getting friendly with shady people and websites.

Refine, refine and refine

Remember that your SEO job is never over. There is always scope for improvement. Imagine that you are maintaining a lawn in your front porch. Maintaining the lawn is a daily job. You have to remove dead links and leaves every single day. You have to cut the lawn once a week or the weeds will overgrow your lawn. Keep adding content to your website every day. Google loves fresh content and it will reward you for it.

Think of new and innovative ideas to attract eyeballs. Participate in offline activities to promote your website. Master the art of email marketing. Work on your social media profile. Your goal must be to get at least fifty new followers every week. Tweet whenever you can.

You should love your website and cherish the content. Search engine optimization is ultimately about details.

Conclusion

SEO domination is all about the process — systematic process. You have to apply the basics and the rest would automatically follow. You must consider Google search algorithm as your friend and not as an enemy. You are not fighting to get into the first page of search engine results. You just have to pip the competition. No more, no less. Here is a roundup of what you have learnt in this book.

Relevancy of your website is an important factor in determining your position in search results. You must provide sufficient reason for Google to consider you as a relevant website. The first step in this direction would be to make your content relevant. Google, for that matter any search engine, is not human. It's an algorithm which tries to mimic human intelligence. Keyword density is an important part of onsite SEO. By the latest count, 2 to 3% keyword density seems to be acceptable to Google. Onsite SEO also takes into consideration how the content is structured. The page title and other factors are factored into the Google algorithm to decide relevancy of your web page.

Smart businesses want to know what their competitors are doing. In management jargon it is known as assessing their strength and weaknesses. In SEO, understanding competitor's strategy is extremely helpful. How do you assess performance of competitors? How do you understand their keyword strategy? How do you know about their web traffic? These inputs can hasten your progress towards website optimization. Let's face it. You don't have to reinvent the wheel. If someone has done it successfully, you must not hesitate to follow in their footsteps.

Your SEO strategy should be top down and there should be coherence throughout your site. When the Google crawler looks at your site, it should find a uniform keyword policy. There should be continuity in your title, description, heading along with content and internal link text. The Google Bot should be able to analyze and suitably index your site for specific keywords. By following this strategy, you would be sending a strong signal to Google – your website is worth a first page ranking.

Creating a content strategy is important. Keywords are important. But when you think about good content everything becomes secondary except the message. Are you providing value to your visitor must be the uppermost question in your mind? Your keyword may have a very low search volume – even five searches a day. It does not matter. Ultimately, the traffic to your site will come from a niche audience who want to read and hear from you.

Measuring and evaluating the success or failure of your SEO effort is important. By doing this you will know what works and what doesn't. You have to keep changing your tactics and align yourself with the trend. What is the point if you attract huge traffic but no one buys from your website? To understand the dynamics of your website, you must watch the trends and developments carefully. You must gather insight into the user experience. You must measure the impact your SEO has on the bottom line.

Social media marketing is increasingly being used for brand and reputation building. You can showcase your brand on various social media channels without seriously damaging your pocket. A lesser known brand can get a boost in search ranking if seriously promoted on social media. Google search algorithm will give you an extra point for each mention on social media. This will get reflected in search results for your brand name.

The best type of SEO is no SEO at all. Forget that you want to appear on the first page of search results. This focus on search results actually takes you away from success. Simply choose a focus keyword and build your content around it. Give it your best shot. Create the best content ever written on the subject. You know more about the subject you are writing about than anyone else in this world.

Do you have confidence in yourself? Do you love your work? SEO will automatically take care of itself if you take care of your content. The secret of SEO is simple enough. This fact has been written about in many books by many experts but we tend to ignore good advice. You think that there must be something which you are missing. Some kind of secret sauce, perhaps! You will be surprised to know that there is no secret sauce after all. Like the Panda in movie 'Kung Fu Panda' says – There is no secret ingredient.

Modern SEO has no rules except one – providing relevant content and presenting it with love. The user is the ultimate decider of your Google ranking. Using social media is a legitimate way to boost traffic to your site. Engage your audience at all levels. Have a top down perspective. See the big picture but don't ignore the details.

SEO domination is nothing but creating value for your customers and visitors to your website. If you catch the wave you will reach there quickly.